The Challenge Center Speaks

January 2014 Edition

Book Structure Technician:
ASA Publishing Company

Coordinator:
Sandy Sigmon
The Challenge Center

Published by:
The Challenge Center
(North Family Community School)

All Rights Reserved. No part of this publication may be reproduced, stored in a retrieval system or transmitted in any form or by any means electronic, mechanical, photocopying, recording, taping, web distribution, information storage, or otherwise, without the without the prior written permission by the Director or the Board of Directors of North Family Community School. Author/writer[s] rights to "Freedom of Speech" protected by and with the "1st Amendment" of the Constitution of the United States of America. This is a work of educational learning purposes. The reader is notified that this text is an educational tool, and the publisher does not assume, and expressly disclaims, any obligation to obtain and include information other than that provided by the author.

Any and all vending sales and distribution not permitted without full magazine cover and this title page.

Copyrights©2014 Sandra Sigmon, (The Challenge Center – *North Family Community School*) All Rights Reserved
Magazine Title: The Challenge Center Speaks
Date Published: 09.2014
Edition: 1 / *January 2014 Edition (Paperback Magazine)*
Book ID: ASAPCID2380658
ISBN: 978-0-578-15135-9
Library of Congress Cataloging-in-Publication Data

This magazine was published in the United States of America.
State of Michigan

TABLE OF CONTENTS

Title	Author	Page
Niki's Story	Sandra J. Sigmon	1
The Most Memorable Christmas	Albertha Brimfield	2
Why People Buy Lottery Tickets	Melissa Sampson	3
My Favorite Song	Williette James	4
Self-Portrait	Julie Ann Jackson	5
Million Dollar	Jaime Jordan	6
That's Why I Love You	Elisa Youmans	7
Self-Portrait	Phillip Wesley Thomas Tooley	8
One of My Favorite Memories	Stephanie Jones	9
My Favorite Music	Alfie Casteal	10
Million Dollar Winner	Brittney Davenport	11
The Mother in Me is You	Elisa Youmans	12
A Waste of Money	Stephone Pettus	13
Pacifiers Versus Thumb-Sucking	Latoya	14
Million Dollars	Ervin Livingston	15
Memorable Christmases	Elisa Youmans	16
My Favorite Song	Stephanie Jones	17
What Would I do If I Won a Million Dollars	Nancy Castillo	18
Learning	John Thompson	19
My Friend	Melissa Sampson	20
Pets	Jaime Jordan	21
Live Life and Find Love	Elisa Youmans	22
My Favorite Memory	Maurice Corbitt	23
How is Your Life Different	Anonymous	24
Self-Portrait	Virginia Rose Chavis	25
If I Had a Million Dollars	Michael Davis	26-27
My Computer	Taylor Lacy	28
Cyber Bullying	Ryan Reeves	29
My Favorite Childhood Memory	Michael Davis	30-31
January	Iva Mack	32
Life	Stepfone Pettus	33
My Favorite Memory	Damon Phillips	34
Memories of an Old Cowboy	George E. Sigmon	35

The Challenge Center Speaks

January 2014 Edition

Niki's Story

When I first saw this pup, I knew I was in trouble. He was in a small cardboard box on the ground at the Flea Market. Niki stood out from the other two pups in the box with his black, red, and white coloring and silky coat. He was so small; he just fit in my hand. I picked him up, turned him around to my husband, and said, "He's stuck to my hand. I cannot put him down. Therefore, my husband said, "Here, let me try." I handed the pup to him and he could not put him down either. The man selling the puppies told me he was eight weeks old and the price was $10. My husband and I each had $5 left, so we bought him.

After we got home, I realized that Niki was only three weeks old and not even weaned. The first night, I fed Niki canned milk mixed with yogurt. I put him to bed in the bedroom with a large stuffed bear, and a hot water bottle, a towel, and a bunny-rattle. This became the routine for more than three weeks. He never cried long before going to sleep, but when the water bottle got cold, he howled. I would have to get up, feed him, and get him warm again.

As Niki got older, we began to realize how smart he was. At two months, he was house broken. He walked on a leash at four months. Niki understood both verbal and silent commands. He was alert and playful all the time. He had an expressive face. I swore sometimes that he laughed at us. His best trick was sitting up, which he did continually. He was always into something. His preferred activity was chewing, especially on my most prized possessions – my books. When I found some of Niki's handiwork, I would show it to him and say in a loud voice "Do you see this?" He would look away from the damaged item, his tail would droop, and he would slink away to hide. He really looked guilty.

All of Niki's most beloved toys and friends began with the letter "B" (except us): Bear, bunny-rattle, ball, bone, bottles, Butterscotch (the cat), and Brianna (Our granddaughter). Niki's favorite toy was his blue ball. In fact, he liked his ball so much that he was nicknamed "Ball Face." He carried his blue ball constantly, wanting us to throw it. He wanted to play ball 24 hours a day. Niki demanded our attention when he had the ball. He would bring the ball to one of us and set it on the floor. If we ignored him, he whimpered or barked. If we still ignored him, he put the ball on the chair or couch next to us and whined. If we still ignored him, he picked the ball up and put it closer, he whined louder. Sometimes, we would point to the spot where we want the ball put, fold our arms, look away from him, and wait. He could not stand it when we ignored him. Eventually, he would put the ball in the exact spot we had pointed to, and then we would pick it up and throw it for him.

Sometimes we hid the ball or other toys. We would tell Niki to "find it." Niki would hunt for the objects until he found them. My husband liked to trick Niki by doing sleight of hand with the ball, moving his hands around until the ball "disappeared." Then, Daddy would put the ball under himself or under a pillow. He told Niki to find it. Niki had learned that if Daddy has the ball, he might be tricking him. Niki would pretend to go behind the couch to look for the ball, but instead would sit where he could watch Daddy. When Daddy moved to throw the ball, Niki came out in a flash and got the ball. Niki learned to tease us, too. Sometimes he would not put the ball down, but would balance the ball between the edge of the couch and his front teeth. He then waited for one of us to notice it. If we tried to grab the ball, he let it drop to the floor, picked it up, and ran away with it.

Niki's favorite little person was our granddaughter, Brianna. She was just two years old and she loved Niki. Brianna and Niki were a match made in heaven. She loved to throw the ball and he loved to fetch it. They would play together all day long. Niki was very gentle with her. He stayed by her side when she ate, so he could clean up the floor. Not all that food fell accidentally I am sure.

Butterscotch (our orange tiger cat) and Niki did not pay much attention to each other when Niki was a pup, but when Niki had gotten more "civilized," they got along well. Niki delighted in chasing Butterscotch across the yard, and then the cat turned around and chased him. In the house, Niki harassed Butterscotch by biting at her tail. She would be patient with him for a while, but when she tired of it that was it. She would grab his face with her claws, flip over on her back, and would bite him on the neck until he whimpered. At that point, she would start grooming him as if he was her kitten. If he tried to move, she would bite him until he was still, and continued grooming him. After a while, if Niki was very still, she would quit grooming him, so he could slowly back away to go lay down somewhere else.

Sometimes my husband or I would throw the ball and it would come to rest next to the cat or under her. Niki would have a fit. He knew that Butterscotch would probably grab him if he tried to pick the ball up with his mouth. Therefore, Niki would slink over to Butterscotch, put his front paw on the ball (as if a cat would), and carefully pull the ball away from the cat, and then he could pick the ball up in his mouth.

Niki had been a delight to our lives, and we have more tales we could tell, but I think you can see why he was so special to us.

By Sandy Sigmon 9-1996 (REVISED 8/2014)

The most memorable Christmas
By Albertha Brimfield

When I was a little girl the most memorable thing I can remember, we were very poor and my mother and father couldn't afford to buy me a doll, but the one thing I can remember is I wanted a doll for Christmas.

I remember getting some silk from an ear of corn to make a doll, I get a soda bottle and tide the silk around the top of the bottle to make hair for my doll drew eyes at the top of the bottle I made a blanket out of a rag to wrap the bottle up so it would look like a baby in a blanket. This was my most memorable Christmas.

Why People Buy Lottery Tickets

I think people buy lottery tickets when they have very little chance of winning because they are addicted to gambling. People also think they have a chance of beating the odds.

Some people get addicted to buying lottery tickets. I know this lady named Beth. She said she likes buying lottery tickets to help with her education funding. Beth said it may be bad by spending a large amount of money, but most of the time it's worth it. Beth said she wins more than she loses. I think that she doesn't know.

Really, I think people buy lottery tickets to take a chance to win. I think it costs too much money. I know a lady name Martha spends her whole paycheck on lottery tickets.

I've tried buying lottery tickets but it's not easy buying lottery tickets every day. I would rather spend money on something my family needs.

Melissa Sampson
3-30-09

My Favorite Song
By: Williette James 11-4-2013

My favorite song is "I See You." I chose this song because when I hear it my soul just lights up. I lost my dad, but this song was not out, then. Now that this song is out, I just sing right along with it. As I sing I am thinking about our old days together. All I can remember are the good things about my dad when he was on earth with me. To me, I know that he is gone but he is not forgotten.

I have a clear mind and a made up my mind after this song came out, that certain parts of the song are important to me. I still can remember a little piece of the song and it goes like this "I see you for all you do, you're not just a face in the crowd. I see you, I see you..."

So, there is a lot to think about as I sing this song to anyone. This song is a really good song not because I said so but just listen to it. You will see for yourself why this is a song I listen to. This song is a good one to use to sit and think about who really means the most in your life. I know my dad really is the most important person in my heart, and it is my conclusion, that this is one of the best songs that Forever Jones has written.

Self Portrait

Hello, my name is Julie Ann Jackson. I am originally from St. Matthews. My mother and I moved to North, when I was fifteen years old. I started attending North High School, and met the wrong crowd. I soon dropped out and moved away from my mother. A few years later, my mother was in a car accident. The car accident altered her life and mine. I turned to drugs and alcohol, until I met someone named Scott Dyches. He was an old friend of mine, and we soon became a couple. He had a few problems as well, so I decided to stay with him and help him. We soon became pregnant, and I had my first child named Savannah Dyches. After I had my first child, we got married. When I became a mother, I became an adult. We now have two more children, a girl named Bethany Dyches, and a boy named Joshua Dyches. My life and choices reflect on my children, so that is why I am here. If I have a better life, they will too.

By: Julie Ann Jackson

12-14-09

MILLION DOLLAR

If I Have a million dollars I help the poor people and then buy me, A new car 1996 v6 Honda Accord lot of video games visit Around the world. New BMX trick Bike. A very nice Home in a very nice neighborhood. Help people all over the work.

Jaime Jordan
2-21-06

That's Why I Love You
By Elisa Youmans

You love me and I no thats true
I feel happiness every time I'm around you
When I look into your eyes my heart melts
Because of feelings it felt
I jump into your arms every time I see you
Because your not just my lover your my boo
You see my stupid past
And are relationship still lasts
You hold my hand when the world hurts me
You listen to my mouth when the world irks me
You hear me say whatever and okay honey
But you know I'm jealous and you think it's funny
You make me so mad sometimes and I could hurt you
BUT......
You love me that's why I love you

Self Portrait

My full name is Phillip Wesley Thomas Tooley. I was born on January 24th 1991 2 months premature. My dad is Darryl Tooley he works at Carpenter Specialty Alloys now for 31 years being a hard worker on the greasy loud machines. My mom works at OC Tech college teaching RN nursing now for 7 years. I have very little family here all my family lives in Greenville. My mom and dad are both from Greenville. I was born in Columbia I live and stay in Orangeburg. I have played baseball my whole life. I have 4 years training mix martial arts fighting. My dad has raised me to be a tough scrapping kid like he was raised. My mom has raised me with the heart. I don't start any trouble I don't pick on anybody I don't cut jokes about people. But if trouble should ever come I  can well protect myself and others. I don't do drugs never have. I don't smoke I do chewing tobacco. If my friends and me go out I might 1 or 2 budlight relaxing. But I don't get all drunk don't get carried away 1 to 2 that's the limit. I do push-ups every morning and night. It don't matter how late it is I do cardio one day push-ups next. I eat a lot of pork-chops also steaks a lot. I cook a lot but healthy food and drink a lot of water. I went to OPS, CA, BA and my favorite Wil Lou Gray. I want to join the Marines until old age. I work, work, work I have had a lot of people say you have to keep Phillip from working over time. I love to workout because makes me feel born again. When the shirt is soaked in sweat and dry heaving you have pushed the limit. It makes me feel like you have accomplished the world a great deal of confidence. I have a girl but she thinks serious I do to sometimes but before that I have things to do in life before that falls into play.

One of My Favorite Memories

One of my most favorite memories occurred around Christmas in 2003. Derek and I had gone to Virginia to spend time with his family for the holidays. It was only the second time I had met his mom's side of the family. They had asked him to come because they were doing family portraits with the whole extended family. This started with his grandparents, then their children, and their children's children. Who knew this trip would change my life.

When we arrived at the portrait studio, everyone was there. They began taking the various family picture poses they wanted. I stood there watching as they decided where to stand and how to arrange the family. Derek's grandmother asked me why I was not with them getting ready for the picture. This surprised me, being it was a family picture, and he and I were only dating. I decided to honor her wishes and became a part of their family photographs. Later that evening there was an annual Christmas party that Derek's uncle held. So we got ready to go to that.

The party had over 100 guests. I did not know very many people, and felt a little uncomfortable. However, I began to have a good time. About halfway through the party Derek called me into the house. I noticed that everyone seemed to be trying to fit into the very small living room. Derek placed me in front of the Christmas tree and I began to wonder what was going on. Then, in front of everyone he got down on one knee. He recited one of the most beautiful speeches I have ever heard, and then asked me to marry him. Of course, I cried and said yes.

I then found out that everyone was in on it, but me. This was the reason they wanted me to join in on the family portraits. They knew that later that night, I would become part of that family. We have now been married for 9 years.

 Stephanie Jones: November 13, 2013

MY FAVORITE MUSIC

My favorite music is a mixture of soulful Hip Hop with a spirit feel. I can call some of it gospel. It affects emotions and soul. The music is very important to me in a song. I look for three things when I hear a song. I listen for a subject, things it make me do, and the ending of a verse. This determines whether I will keep listening. I love for my music to have live instruments. All of my music and lyrics are divinely inspired. When I'm involved in music, I feel the true holy spirit of Jehovah, GOD. Emotionally, I tear up because of the feeling I get. Most of the time I'm remembering a moment of being and giving my time to God for all His creations. Sometimes I feel like the one angel, Lucifer, and the strength of cheribims.

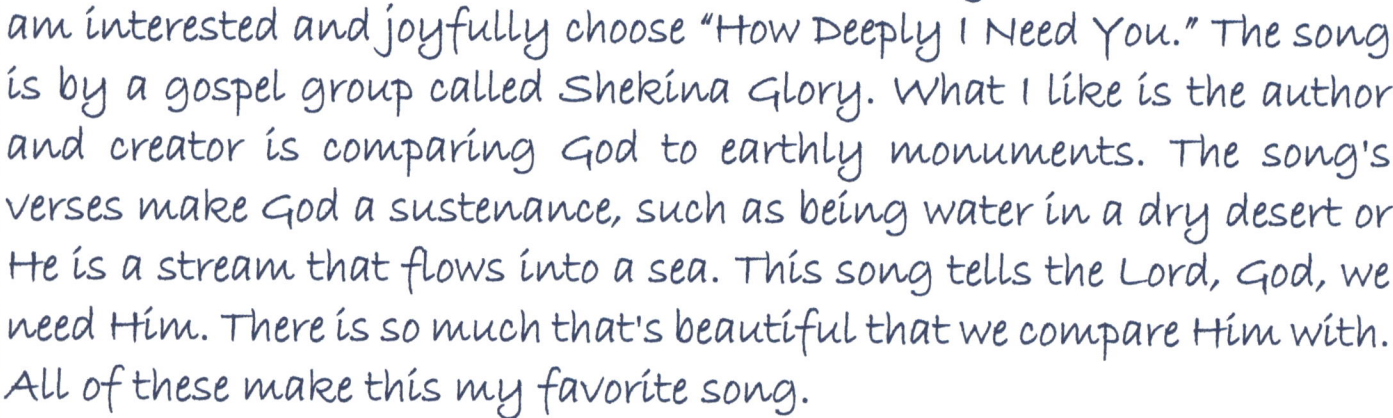

I make my own music because it is a true part of me and my favorite hobby. My favorite music is an expression of combined sounds and flavor in my ear. I am interested and joyfully choose "How Deeply I Need You." The song is by a gospel group called Shekina Glory. What I like is the author and creator is comparing God to earthly monuments. The song's verses make God a sustenance, such as being water in a dry desert or He is a stream that flows into a sea. This song tells the Lord, God, we need Him. There is so much that's beautiful that we compare Him with. All of these make this my favorite song.

      Alfie Casteal 10-30-2013

Million Dollar Winner

If I won a million dollars I would move to the beach and take acting, something I've always wanted to do.

I would move my family to the beach, maybe the Pacific Coast. I love the way the Pacific Coast looks with all the foothills and exotic plants and trees. I would buy a fix me up house and fix it up in my own style with three bedrooms and two bathrooms. I would add an open kitchen with attached living room. The house would be a two stories with bright colors and big rooms.

The other thing I would do is take acting lessons. I've always pictured myself on a stage somewhere doing a drama or something or maybe even a movie. I've been an extra once or twice but that wasn't good enough for me. I want to have an exciting movie or Broadway career, not to make a name for myself but because I enjoy doing such.

I'm a quiet person, but I have another side of me that likes to come out and she's a bright, bubbly, focused, and ambitious person. Not a day goes by that I don't see myself on a beach with my family doing what I love being an actress, mother, and wife. That's what I would do if I won a million dollars.

Brittney Davenport
10-02-2013

The Mother in Me is You

I stand strong when no one is looking
I look beautiful without trying
Seeing right through that mischievous smile of that red headed baby girl
I see every regret in that child's heart and I don't love her any less
I see her mistakes and I never judge her
I see the imperfections of her body and to me they make her perfect
My baby girl experiments but after each time she grows up a little more
Little baby girl follows in mommy's shadow because mommy is her hero
I get my happiness by seeing my little baby girl achieve her goals
Baby girls best friend is mommy
I rest easy knowing my baby girl has grown up and has been inspired by me
Baby girl looks beautiful without trying
Baby girl stands strong when no one is looking

By: Elisa Youmans

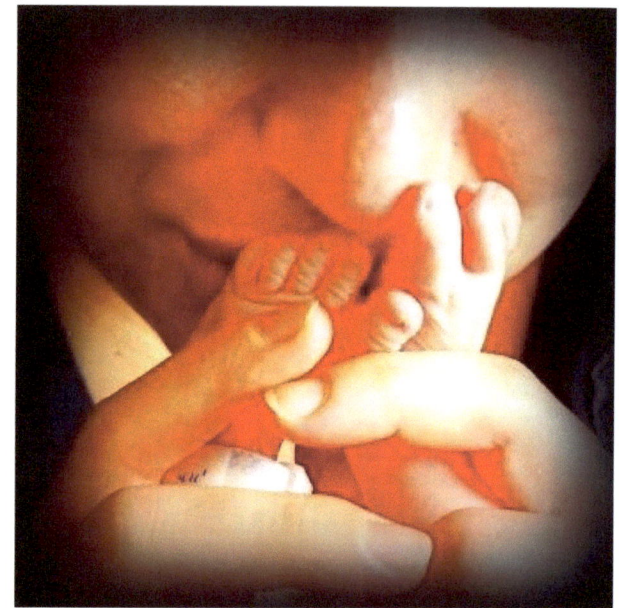

A Waste of Money

Many people buy lottery tickets even though they have very little chance of winning. The jack pot is so high people think they have a chance at winning. People get hooked on buying the tickets.

People love big money; they see the lottery as a giveaway. Little do they know hitting the jack pot is a one and a million chance. My friend buys tickets all the time but never wins anything.

People get hooked like a kid looking at new shoes. Some people always want more lottery tickets. My dad always has to buy tickets.
Some people get 5 to 6 tickets and might win a dollar.

To me, people mess up by spending a lot of money on tickets every day. If someone did hit, they wouldn't even get all of the jack pot. I wouldn't waste my money on lottery tickets.

.by: stepfone pettus
date: april 20, 2009

Pacifiers Versus Thumb-sucking

Many parents may think that using pacifiers and thumb-sucking is the same thing but it's not. They both have their own pros and cons. They can help and hurt your child in various ways.

The pros of thumb-sucking are you don't have to buy it, it can never get lost, and it is an easier way of comfort. You don't have to spend any money on numerous amount of pacifiers. The children have their own access to it. The parents don't have to stop what they are doing to comfort the child in getting the thumb. Parents don't ever have to worry about looking for it.

The cons of thumb-sucking is that it can cause severe teeth damage. It would be very hard to stop or wean a child off of thumb-sucking. In the long run the children will have severe tooth damage such as, rotten of the teeth, and buck teeth. Their teeth may become buck, which means they would be pushed toward the front. They may need braces in the long haul, and that becomes very expensive for the parents. A huge over bite is also common in thumb-sucking. It could also cause a child to have a slurred speech. Children who suck their thumb also have social problems, they may be teased or bullied. It can cause infections and peeling of the skin.

Pacifiers are also effective when it comes to comforting a child. You may be able to take away the pacifier from the child. Parents can limit the access children have to them. A pacifier can be a replacement from the bottle. It helps the child to soothe down and it shows comfort. It also gives them a sense of relief.

The cons of pacifiers are that children get addicted to them. They feel as if they gotta have it. This is a bad sign because children may just act out just to get the pacifier. Their teeth also may get buck with the pacifier. They may also get rotten teeth from staying on the pacifier too long. The pacifier may keep the children quiet but if on them too long it will hurt children. If not kept clean it to can cause infections and illnesses.

The pros and cons of both pacifiers and thumb-sucking are mostly the same. They basically cause the same health problems. Some may cost you a little more money than others. They both are used to comfort and soothe the children. They both are used to make a child feel a sense of security.

One fact stated that African American mothers favor using a pacifier or physical stimulation in response to crying, while Euro-American parents use physical touch and holding, Cuban Americans mothers use a combination of both the pacifiers and cuddling.

Latoya 2008

Million Dollars

If I won a million dollars, I want to become famous on Hollywood film and buy a new van.

Why do I want to be on film? I fell in love with film directing, but I have actually never experienced film. I want to know how to direct films. I am willing to pay for everything. I, myself, will work hard for success, because my path must find a thoughtful way. No matter what I do, I must believe that what I do is true. I have to struggle for everything I try to do.

I want to buy a new van. It is very important for carrying my special wheelchair. My van will be gray and smooth. It will have technical controls and buttons for things. The van will be a large size.

That's what I would do with a million dollars.

Ervin Livingston
10/16/13

Memorable Christmases
by Elisa Youmans

I have many memorable Christmases, not one in specific. I can tell you many things I loved about these Christmases while they lasted for several years of my life.

On Christmas morning, my sister and I would get up and wake up are my mom and dad. When my sister and I finally get my mom dad up, we would go open all are presents. Then my sister and I would give are mom and dad there presents from us.

When we got all are presents opened, my sister and I got up and got dressed. Mom and Dad did also. When all of us were ready to go, we would help Momma put all the food she prepared in her car. Then we helped Daddy put the turkey and oil in his truck. We are going to grandma's house.

When we got to grandma's house we unloaded Mom's car and Dad's trunk. We went inside grandma's house and gave are family hugs and kisses. We also waited and more family to come while my dad cooked the turkey.

When all the family had arrived the turkey was finished. Daddy cut up the turkey and everybody fixed a plate. We all ate the good food each family member fixed and caught up in each other's lives.

Christmas like these were the best for my first fourteen years of my life. Now I am sixteen and my sister has moved out and my grandma and my grandpa are in the nursing home. Christmases are spent with mom and dad at our house. All I can say from this memory is that life is precious and don't take people for granted because everything and everyone could be gone in a split second.

My Favorite Song

My favorite song is a song that is formally named *Skin*, but is often referred to as *Sarabeth*. There are several reasons that this song is so special to me. The first thing is I had a daughter who was born with a disease, and this song is about a girl with cancer. Another thing is the girl in the song and my daughter have the same name, Sarabeth. Yet another is that it came out around the time my daughter was born. The song *Skin (Sarabeth)* is my favorite song because it reminds me of my daughter, and shows me how things could have been if she had survived her disease.

Rascal Flatts sings this song and it is about a teenage girl who goes to the doctor and finds out she has cancer. It explains that she is scared. It also has some detail about what she goes through with treatment and losing her hair, and the insecurity this causes her. Around the time I found out my daughter had a rare disease is when I first heard this song. The nurses' taking care of her told me to listen to it. This song instantly reminded me of her. Even though there were differences in their situations.

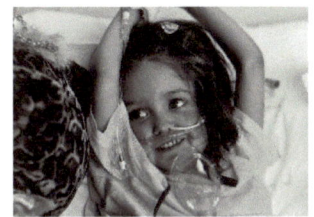
My Daughter Sarabeth

My daughter was only 3 months old, while the girl in the song was a teenager. The girl in the song had cancer, and my child had a liver disease. My daughter passed away, and the girl in the song survived. The lyrics of the song, despite the differences still make me think of my Sarabeth every time I hear it. This song also shows me what could have been.

The Sarabeth in the song is insecure because the treatments caused her to lose her hair, and she thought no boy would want to take her to the prom. At the age of 3 my daughter was already insecure about the many scars she had. The girl in the song is greeted at the door by her date, whom has shaved his head to match hers. I like to imagine my daughter growing up and having someone make a similar gesture to ease her insecurities.

This song touches me every time I hear it. You may see me driving down the road crying, because it is playing on my radio. Although the situations were different, the similarities are many. The fact of the shared name makes me feel like this song was meant to help me through this hard situation in my life. I would say that by far this is one of my most favorite songs.

My name is Stephanie Jones. I am 32 years old, and the mother of 2 children. One being the daughter that I lost that this essay refers to. I also have a 6 year old son. I am happily married to my best friend and just celebrated our 9th wedding anniversary.

11/11/2013

What Would I do if I Won a Million Dollars

If I won a million dollars I would give some to the missionaries at my church and I would give some to my children.

The reason I am going to give money to the missionaries at my church is because they will help families that are in need. They will have everything that they need. I do this because when I moved out here from New York the church help me with everything to get on my feet so I want to pay it forward by helping a family in need to get on their feet.

The reason I'm giving money to my son, Manuel, is so he can buy a house and open a business. If he has a business and a house, he can always have a secure place for him and his family. He wouldn't have to live his life the way I did. I was moving all the time. I never had a steady place to live. For my daughter, Stefanie, and her family I would also buy her a house and a small business for her husband. This way he would always be able to support his family. For my other daughter, Nia, I would also buy her a house and a car. This way she would always have a place to live and be secure. A car would help her get back and forth to work as a house nurse.

The reason I do these things is because it brings such big joy to my heart. I would have accomplished one of my goals in life. I can help others the way I was helped by my church.

Nancy Castillo 10-16-13

Learning

I am thinking positively now instead of thinking negatively about learning. I am learning  to spell words and pronounce words. And I am learning to know the meaning of the words. I am writing about sentences and learning the words and meaning of both. I am learning to prove words and pronounce them better.

John Thompson

12-1-013

> I am a Vietnam veteran. I am a welder and a truck driver. I am starting to enjoy school where I didn't before.

My Friend

On February 6, 2009, I saw this lady walking around town. We stopped to see her one day. I asked her if she needed a ride; she said no thank you. Every time I would go to town, she would always be walking. She is very nice. She doesn't mind helping people or being around other people. When I arrive at school, she's there doing her work or watching the door at times. She is always smiling or talking about class work. I think she is the best person to be around.

This lady is short. She keeps herself looking nice. She's always doing something to keep herself busy. I would never hear this lady complain about anything. Her hair is not too long and not too short. She keeps it curled up. This lady no matter where she sees you she always speaks. There is no one that could take this lady's place. I don't really know her hobbies, but she loves to walk.

The person I'm writing about is Albertha.

Melissa Sampson 03-10-09

Pets

The subject of this essay is a comparison of five different types of pets. I will describe the following pets: dogs, spiders, birds, rabbits, and fish. Dogs are just like people. Dogs are living longer today than they have in the past. Immunizations have eliminated many of the serious diseases of the past such as distemper and heart worms. I think dogs make better pets because they are more playful. Dogs can be noisy.

A young spider stands on tip toe at the top of a grass stem. With his abdomen tilted upwards it weaves a fine silk strand into the breeze. The silk rises in the warm air and soon exerts a strong pull on the animal. The spiderling lets go and drifts up into the air, carried aloft by its thread. Tarantulas are interesting pets because they are different. I wouldn't want one for a pet because many people are scared of spiders- including me!

Sometimes a drastic change in the weather will kill the food crops, causing the birds to starve to death. A change in climate can leave the bird population prey to hungry predators. I would like to have a bird for a pet because they are a part of nature and they can fly high into the sky. Also, birds can be messy and hard to clean up after.

Rabbits as pets are harmless, friendly, and robust. They breed quite easily and may be kept indoors or outdoors year round. I think rabbits make a great pet because they are harmless. Also the well nigh impossible job of keeping wild rabbits is a real challenge to any pet keeper.

Fish have lived on earth longer than any other back-boned animals and show greater diversity in their ways of life. If interest in fish can be judged by interest in fishing, they are the most popular animals. I would like to have a fish for a pet because they are fun to watch and they have so many colors. The hardest thing to me about keeping a fish for a pet is to clean the fish bowl and change the water.

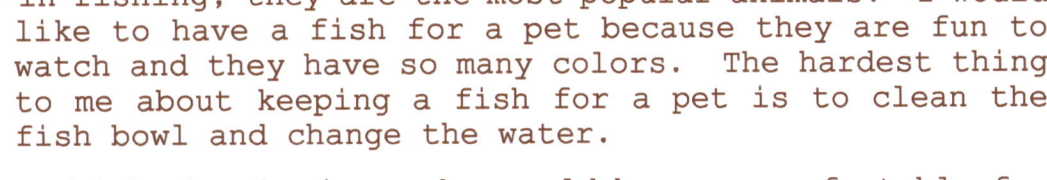

I think that having a dog would be more comfortable for me. I think they make great pets.

By: Jamie Jordan   10-29-2009

Live Life & Find Love

My love you are so great,
you make my heart never want to hate.

You say my body is so wonderful,
you make me feel like I could be center-fold.
People look at you and say he will never be anything,
I look at them and say he is my everything.
Everyone sees are struggles and hard times now
but, when we climb to the top everyone will be like wow.
I think you deserve the best,
but, you tell me you want me and none of the rest.
One day all are dreams will come true
and our lives will excel like we never knew.
One day we will become one
and we bring into the world two,
and are love will forever stay true.

2/13/09 til 4ever
we will be 2gether
Elisa Youmans & Jr Canaday

My Favorite Memory

My favorite memory is graduating high school. I use to enjoy going to North High School. I had a lot of fun attending North High. I played football and basketball my four years of school. I was also a member of VICA club and FCA club. I was an honor roll student. I studied very hard and was dedicated to doing my homework. I really miss those days. They were some of the best years of my life. It would be nice to meet my teachers and classmates to see how they doing. My favorite teacher is Mr. Donaldson. He made me into the man I am today. Without Mr. Donaldson I don't know where I would be now. He was like a father figure to me. I really enjoyed being in carpentry class. We use to do all kinds of things. We laid bricks for a foundation. We also use the table saw to cut wood. We made floats for the homecoming and Christmas parades. We attended the VICA convention my four years of school. The convention was on the weekend and we went to the Marriott hotel in Columbia.

The convention was very exciting and amazing. U got to meet new people. The first night all the schools met in the lobby for the opening ceremony. Saturday morning we competed in different competitions. Saturday night was award night and when that was over it was a reception in the ballroom. The two days at the VICA convention was very engaging and wonderful. I loved being in typing class with Mrs. Bellingham. She was the nicest lady you met on the planet. She would let us get on the computer when we finished our assignment. Typing class was very fun and I could not wait for it to begin. I thought the class would be a drag, but it was a blast. Mrs. Bellingham was a great teacher and she is very good at what she does. I also loved being in tech prep English class taught by Mrs. Cave. She was very polite to all of her students. She would always help u if you had a problem. If u were having a bad day she would make u laugh and forget about your situation. She is also someone u would like to meet because she has a great personality. My football coach Tony Felder was the best football coach ever. He was very dedicated to his coaching staff and players. He made football practice fun and you did not wanted to go home. He is a good motivator  and would inspire us to play football every Friday night. I loved football it was a competitive sport. It was exciting to step on the gridiron. Getting to hit your opponent was the greatest feeling ever. Scoring touchdowns was so amazing. Hearing the crowd cheer would have us fired up ready to play. Winning games was also sweet. We practiced our tails off to strive to be a better team. Playing each game for forty-eight minutes was grueling but it was exceptional.

My name is Maurice Corbitt. I live in a small town of North South Carolina. I work nights in Pelion South Carolina at WP Rawls. I love to come up to the Challenge Center in North South Carolina. Mrs. Sandy and Mr. George are the nicest people you'll ever meet. I come up here to get on the computer. The Challenge Center is a great place. If you are ever in North come and stop by here and you will have a terrific time.

                            Maurice Corbitt   12/11/2013

How is your Life Different because he lived?

My life is different in many ways because of Dr. Martin Luther King, Jr. I was able to be born into a generation of peace. In his generation, people were to love certain people. He made a change in that, therefore; I was taught to love all people. He showed me the meaning of loving one another. He taught me, everyone is equal. He proved to me, things are possible through non-violence, rather than violence.

-Anonymous-

January 19, 2010

Self Portrait

My name is Virginia Rose Chavis. I got my Name from my grandmother and mom. Virginia is my grandmother's name. Rose is my mother's middle name. I was born in Orangeburg, South Carolina on May 13, 1992. I am my mother and father's first born out of 2. My parents are deaf. So, I had to learn sign language. I started when I was 2 years old. I have one brother he is 2 years younger than me. We are just a like. He still attends school tho. I am a pet lover. I have plenty of animals. I am quite. I can't learn in a loud environment. That's why I dropout of High school. I don't like nosy people. I am very friendly. Given up is not what I like to do. I work hard. And I plan to get my GED and finish school.

Virginia Rose Chavis
(and she did it too!)

If I Had A Million Dollars

Everyone has a different view of the balance between being financially successful and how they give back to their community. The best way I can describe the way I feel about this situation can be portrayed by a song I heard last week. A portion of the song says, "If I had a million dollars, I'd be rich." Not only would I be rich financially, but I would be rich and enriched with the good feelings I would get from giving back to the community. Many financially gifted people, mostly public figures, tend to give back to the communities they grew up in or live in. I am from the Indianapolis area and lately many people have been actively giving back. For instance, Peyton Manning just visited my old elementary school for a charity event, Jeff Gordon had his annual charity bowl, and Tony Stewart's foundation funded the new cheetah exhibit at the Indianapolis Zoo. Financially blessed people not only give back to the community with their money but by also just have fellowship with their community members. I can't think of many little kids who would rather meet or hang out with their favorite athlete for a day than earn a sum of money.

It doesn't really matter what position you hold. If you are a successful person, people will look up to you. This is true in your office or in your community. So if you are blowing your nose with hundred dollar bills instead of using your money for a good purpose, it will come across that you could care less about the people who live around you and helped you get to where you are in life. After all, people who are always giving back and are active in their communities are the ones people look up to and often call "heroes." I feel this is best represented by the recent situation involving NBA star LeBron James. He was considered a hero in Cleveland, Ohio. He was born there, and was "supposed" to be the chosen one to bring a national title to the city. He was active in his community and loved by more than he was hated by. But when he announced he was going to sign with Miami, many people hated him throughout the nation for either not staying in Cleveland or for not signing with the team they liked, although the fact of the matter was he was taking less money for what he believed in and for the opportunity to bring the Miami community something great.

    As you can see from these examples there are a wide spectrum of ways an individual can balance their finances and what they can do for their community. Even a person making $30,000 a year can donate their time to different charitable organizations such as the Red Cross, food banks, or picking up trash on the side of the road. But the big picture is not what one person does in their community but how everyone working together can make a big impact on the other people that live around them. After all, President John F Kennedy said, "it is not what your country can do for you, but what you can do for your country."

By Michael Davis
12/18/13

My Computer

My computer has affected me in a good way. It has helped me with school. It has also helped me with learning on instruments, because I play guitar and piano.

When I need to write an essay, and I forgot what order it is supposed to go in, I just go on the Internet and look up how to do it. It has also helped me with my typing abilities. I can now type 45 words per minute!

The computer has also helped me with my instrumental abilities. Just by going on "Youtube.com", I can look up "how to play". I learn the song in less than a day. Without my computer, I wouldn't know as many melodies as I do today.

Without my computer, I wouldn't be as smart, or even have my good grades like I do today. I also wouldn't have my musical repertoire that I have learned from the computer.

By: Taylor Lacy Feb. 1, 2012

Cyber Bullying

In this new age of computers the bullies have gone high tech and now are called cyber bullying. There are two ways to stop cyber bullying. One way is tell an adult what is going on. The second way is tell them to stop picking on you.

If someone is bullying online you tell an adult what is going on. Like if is bullying on the internet and calling you names. My friend John Thomas was been bullied on Facebook by some people, so he told them to stop or he was go call the law and they stop bullying him.

The next way is to tell the bullies to stop picking on you. If he or she is bullying you tell them to stop. If they do not stop, tell an adult or the law. My friend Jeremy was going to school and get was bullying for his size and weight. He told them to stop. They came bullying him so told the teacher Mrs. Smith and the bullying stop.

I have been picked on and bullyied in school, but I have never been cyber bullyied. Cyber bullying is a new way of picking on people. I do not like it at all.

By: Ryan Reeves   11/20/2013

My Favorite Childhood Memory

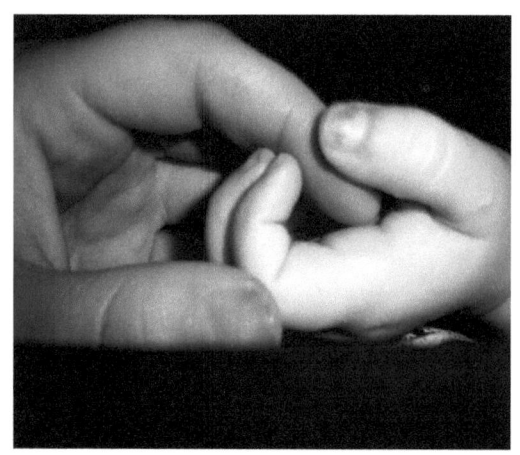

'Tis obvious that all of our childhood memories are not accidental... When you are a child every scent, every sound, every move, every toy, the first day of school, the first kiss, the first step. Everything together makes what is the personality of a man. All these are pieces of one whole entity. I was sitting and thinking – which of the memories I have is the brightest and most emotional for me.... Is it the day when I stayed home alone for the first time? Is it the day when I was so disappointed with the Christmas gift I got? Or maybe when I broke grandma's favorite vase and put it back together with glue? I was thinking about good memories and bad memories... moments of tears and moments of innocent joy. From one memory to another my heart started to feel strange and I felt really strange – like I was in a completely another dimension which exists only in my head. And then. BANG! I got it so clear that I started shivering...

I was about 6 years. My mom's best friend left to another town and asked my mom to stay at her place with me for two days in order to look after her two sons. One was a little older then I was, and the second boy appeared to be super grown-up for he was already fourteen. I always enjoyed staying at their place – a lot of toys, a lot of space, video games – everything a child needs to free the most sincere smile. I remember the second day we were supposed to have the com-back party for my mom's friend at here place…I woke up. Mom went to work and reminded me to be nice and clean by the time she will come back with the guests. I stayed with Tony, the older of the boys and suddenly somebody called him and though he was not permitted to leave me alone – he left. He said he would not be long….but it took him forever…I realized that I am alone… I cannot come out of the house…so I opened the window and thought that I was joking. And I was so desperate…so lonely…so betrayed… at that moment I pulled the curtain so strongly that I fell on the floor. And there I was standing – one little criminal…Desperate to escape and knowing that I will be punished for destroying the curtain that was not even ours….

But then something changed…I stopped whining…looked around and realized that I am in a safe place… that mom will come back and kiss me no matter what I have done. This was a moment of pure happiness…not the happiness of getting a new toy…or a dog. A going to the party of your best friend. It was the moment of clarity for me…the first time in my life when I realized that I am happy to have my mom and that I am safe. My eyes saw the world in different shades that moment. And by the way – I was not punished for the curtain… I felt asleep on my mom's knees.

By Michael Davis

January 13-2004 Iva Mack

One Sunday moring we had sun school. When we finsh sun school. We have five mines. Then we to to serve. We sing and pray. Sunday af noon we went to Mt. Pleasant.

November, 14, 2003

What's the nicest thing anyone has done for you?

When I had my heart attack my friend he leave NY to come to SC. And he left that evening I had the heart attack that night. Someone called him and told him so he turned right around and came back.

Life

Life, if I was white or black,
Life, would not take any slack.
If I can be born again,
I'll do it in the same skin I am in.

To let my grandma's love die - no, not I!
I'll stay around and let love fly,
Noting in this world could feel so warm
Or treats so sweet as grandma's love !

Life throws all kind of twist and turns.
You learn something new every day, I was told.
You should never say life is dull,
Life is not what we take - it's what we give.

By Stepfone Pettus 11,25,2008

My Favorite Memory

My favorite memory is of spending Christmas with my family. My dad and I went to Columbia to my aunt's house. We had gotten there a little late. When we got there all my cousins and their wives and my little cousins were there. My uncle was on the way. When I got there I started playing with my little cousins. My aunt was cooking some pies, ham, macaroni and cheese, green beans, and other stuff. My older cousins were in the living room watching a movie. My dad and uncle were outside around the fire. Then it was time to eat. Everybody sat down, we said grace and ate all the food. It was really good. Then we exchanged some presents. We watched my little cousins open their presents. My dad and I hugged everybody, told everyone bye. Then we went home.

By Damon Phillips 1/20/14

Memories of an Old Cowboy

One of my fondest memories I have as a child was one Christmas, it had to be in the early 50's. I had been to a small drug store on the Patapisco Avenue near our house.  I saw a set of cap pistols in holsters for sale on the top shelves. I could see myself on Christmas morning with that set of guns strapped on my hips shooting up the neighborhood.

The guns were buntline specials, which Wyatt Earp used in a TV program at that time. The guns had pearl handles and 8 inch barrels which could shoot straighter and farther than a 6 inch barrel. The guns cost almost 10 dollars. My mom and dad did buy the set of guns for me for Christmas and a box of caps. I was very happy to go out that morning to show of my new guns, the best on the block. I won many gun fights that year because I had guns that shot straighter and further than any set of guns on the block.

This is a very fond memory of my youth, but I have had many memorable occasions in my life. This is only one

The fastest gun in the neighborhood in the 50's
George E. Sigmon

www.ingramcontent.com/pod-product-compliance
Lightning Source LLC
Chambersburg PA
CBHW041535040426
42446CB00002B/98